Kim Addonizio writes, 'All poems
cause I'm spellbound by this collec
and all Nashville, teeming with ligh
bonds that bind and break us, child   ...., curvy bodies,
and desirous bodies that destroy and are destroyed by lovers. Here, colors are vi-
brant with 'pussy pinks and rent-paying reds.' Lips kiss scars, and at the seam of
every poem is a deep longing and a refusal, a reaching after the hard mythologies
that try to define us, but never do. *Lilith, but Dark* glows in the night."

—Tiana Clark, author of *Equilibrium*

They say my people/ collectively fear water,' suggests our drowning risk and
love hungry speaker in 'Underwater.' And yet Nichole Perkins' *Lilith, but
Dark* is a reservoir of poems defined by 'a blue that never stops' and 'a blue I
never wanted.' Despite whatever fear, Perkins floats us deep into this southern
basin and its deposits of family violence, boys and babies lost too young, skin
scarred by eros or its lack. But these are not studies in brokenness. Rather they
are poems rich with the complications and conundrums and power of one
modern blk womanhood, agile- and able-voiced. For all we know, the storied
Lilith (in all her unwillingness to supplicate before Adam) may have been dark.
But if you could not consider, could not hear, such a notion before reading
this collection, you will see it vividly as Perkins refuses to lift the weight of her
verses from your breast, where they 'press a symphony from you.'"

—Kyle Dargan, Cave Canem Prize winner & author of *Anagnorisis: Poems*

There is a woman here, heady and blooming' reads the last line of the last
poem in this astonishing collection. And there is a woman here, heady and
blooming in each of these infinitely resonant poems. With poise and precision,
Nichole Perkins lays bare a black woman's life, her love, her loss—how she has
come apart and pulled herself back together, how she has wanted and been
wanting. There is so much beautiful writing to be found in these pages, such
fine attention to detail, such a seductive way of imbuing each line and verse
with intimacy and wisdom, so that we always understand how time and place
have shaped the poet and the unforgettable way she renders this world."

—Roxane Gay, author of *Difficult Women*

"In *Lilith, but Dark*, we find a woman 'born armored against…loss,' who, over the course of the collection, lowers her shield, lets it hang "too loosely." Perkin deftly navigates the risks that come with lowering one's protections, of seeing and be seen, with grace and generosity. In the world of the collection— a Southern space, a vulnerable place— her speaker rises, a woman marked by desire, by envy, by family, by love."

—DONIKA KELLY, AUTHOR OF *BESTIARY*

"Nichole Perkins is a myth maker, and the poems in *Lilith, but Dark* swirl with the urge to divine animals from the clouds and constellations from freckles. In this book, everything is a story, a caravan of history, woven together with the smallest, most exquisite observations. These poems make myths from the crayon haze of childhood, familial and romantic relationships, antiquity, and everything in between. I love that the work acknowledges the construction inherent in recollection, that 'Fictions teach us our grief should bruise the sky, while still letting us get lost in the lyrics. These poems are a communion, and I am so delighted with the new animals and constellations Nichole has given us

—TOMMY PICO, AUTHOR OF *IRL*

LILITH, BUT DARK

First published by Publishing Genius in 2018
Atlanta, GA
publishinggenius.com

ISBN 978-1-945028-14-4

Book design by Adam Robinson
Also visit nicholeperkins.com, Tweet @tnwhiskeywoman

LILITH, BUT DARK

NICHOLE PERKINS

PUBLISHING
GENIUS PRESS

Poems

To my mother, sister, and brother, who always believed

Sylvan Park Elementary

We lived between Fisk and Tennessee State.
My new school wasn't far from Vanderbilt.
Red-headed, freckled girls
cheated from me then asked
how I got in the gifted class.
Blond girls brought green things to lunch.
I had a little orange ticket.
These girls Band-Aids were made for
always asked to share my pizza.

I sat with Ellie and Maggie,
Holly and Sara at lunch.
They'd smirk at my bus partners
at their separate table.
Every day, Nakia and Tee-Tee,
Patricia and Rotunda showed all their teeth
when I joined them at recess.
The Band-Aid girls played
silly shit like Castle,
pretending to be asleep until a prince—
always another girl; boys weren't allowed—
kissed them awake.
But us bussed-in girls,
we played with boys,
throwing them down hills made with
smooth, playground gravel,
brown-gold like some of us,
laughing when they grabbed
our ankles and we fell,

our mothers' ponytail artwork
unraveling as we did,
real live Jacks and Jills,
broken crowns and stinging pink-white knees,
our eyes closed from joy,
never in hopes of rescue.

soft

years ago,
earrings were mounted on velvet,
even if bought from woolworth's.
my aunt would detach the fabric
and rub her thumb over it repeatedly,
while sucking her tongue, its tip visible between her lips.

she kept the habit until death—
mother of a teenage son, malignant cantaloupes
pulled from her abdomen,
painlessness found in the tufted luxury
under a thumb.

For Bobby

10/22/31- 3/16/2008

They had to break his jaw to close his mouth.
It was strange to see the tightly-closed smile on his face,
an unnatural "U," shaped into unfamiliar paleness.
It didn't look peaceful at all.
Theresa thought they'd done a good job.

At Christmas, his eyes were searching.
"Willa?"
No, Gran'daddy. It's me.
He picked through memories and ghosts,
held her hand more tightly.

She'd run into the house, looking for him,
her white, hard-bottomed shoes barely touching carpet.
There he was— a grin opening the brown of his face.
She'd curl up in his arms, pretending to understand golf,
then fall asleep, taking his scent with her to darkness.

When My Brother Was Little

He liked to carry sticks.
They had to be a certain length and thickness.
Only he knew the precise length and thickness.
My neighbor watched my brother have a conversation with himself
and said how freeing it must be to live in a private world.
Every Sunday I prayed God would make him normal.

When my brother was little,
he loved He-Man, Voltron, Superman, and the Incredible Hulk.
He would put together the Voltron lions
and sit the super robot creation in its own chair.
If you moved it, his cries would peel the walls down around us.
My brother pretended to be He-Man and punched holes
in those walls. He would hide this evidence of strength
behind masking tape that blended perfectly.
He was clever and sneaky like any other boy.

My brother is a grown man now.
He still loves superheroes,
especially the ones that get to break free
of their skin.

berserker

He barged through the house,
eyes shined to a polish
by big-bottled beer,
beating his chest
and then my mother's.

When I return to this scene,
I can stop him.
In my dreams,
I've come loaded for bear
and shoot a hole
through the fistprint
over his heart.
In my dreams,
no one cares
that I look like him.

I have saved us all.

For a Tree Is Known by Its Fruit

Take the nose.
It's his.
These hands—
Where can I exchange them?
He wrote, too, for a while,
but don't take that from me.
I need the skill to ground me.
With each stretch and sway,
life will open in my new hands.
I hope they never curl into fists.

On Red and Blue Foam

The teacher turned off the lights and left the room.
When she'd return,
she'd smell of burnt milk and sugar,
her fingertips of flame and spit.

Before she'd leave,
we'd close our eyes too tightly,
lids twitching, fingers jumping.
    She didn't care.
Even after the door snicked,
we girls kept our eyes closed,
licked our lips cooled dry from muted hope.

Pierre, Mississippi-red Pierre,
his hair curled tight onto his scalp,
a pineapple of sandy kinks,
kissed us.
He'd circle the room three, sometimes four, times.
A hand on our foreheads, his lips sideways,
our mouths became rough, giggly crosses.

After the second day of nap time kisses,
he brought in a handkerchief his grandfather said all men should carry
He'd wipe his mouth between girls—a gentleman in the making.

A Kind of Rainbow

One of the trailer park girls went home early,
her face gingham-patched with shame,
her shirt sleeves pulled over her hands
so she could rub the heels of her palms
against her head.

The next day, the teacher wore gloves
and used a pencil to part the hair
of children who colored themselves Peach.
I mixed Burnt Sienna and Indian Red
to find a shade for my skin.

When the girl next to me returned to her seat,
I stood for my turn.
The teacher adjusted the gloves at her wrists,
looked away, told me to sit back down.

My face bloomed Mahogany.

The girl next to me marveled that I could blush, too.

Tamara

Tamara was the Flo-Jo of elementary school.
If you were lucky,
you'd catch a glimpse of her trailing hair
before she reached the finish line.
The boys constantly challenged her,
pushing the endpoint farther and farther,
demanding she tie her hair back,
no, leave it loose,
now run barefoot.
Stupid, stupid boys.

Tamara lived in a place where
you sometimes had to run barefoot,
in the dark,
running until your grandmother pressed
a cool cloth against your forehead
and gave you a nip of the special hot tea
something told her to make for you.
The tea tasted funny and strong
and smelled a little like the reason you ran,
but it allowed you to fall asleep
with your grandmother's hand on your chest,
pushing peace into your heart.

The boys would line up to race Tamara,
giving her no rest between.
She knew how to pace,
knew how to hold her breath and disappear.
Those boys were nothing.

When she beat them all,
there was always one who'd yell in her face
and try to push her down,
but Tamara knew how to deal with that, too.
She never got in trouble.
The teachers,
with their mouths slashing their faces,
their bright, angry eyes,
never sent Tamara home.

Tokens

My sister stared at the sky,
claimed it was "Saturday blue,"
made for picnics and aimless walks.

The hearse eased through neighborhoods.
We followed quietly, our destination clear,
watching as strangers paused along the roadside,
offered peace with bowed heads and signs of the cross.
Some kissed their fingertips then tossed the blessing up
to God, to the man going in the ground— I don't think anyone knew.
A mid-day construction crew pressed hard hats against their chests
and remained that way until we could no longer see them.

Fictions teach us our grief should bruise the sky
and send cold rains to echo our misery.
Maybe the lost want to send us a cloudless sky,
filled with a blue that never stops.

A Light Sleeper, Now

I think I heard him —
his last breath.
It shook me awake, but only for a second.
The dark was cotton against my eyes.

The alarm on his sleep machine sounded.
No more need for continuous air.
The better night's rest is eternal now.
Do you think he reached for me?

I bought a new mattress,
now I wake up every time
bunnies pass through the yard.
I watch them from the kitchen window.
They might need me.

Mother-Daughter Ritual

When we were younger,
she'd sit on the floor
between my knocked knees,
no pillow beneath her,
and tease me about my monkey feet.
She'd direct me to the really itchy spots
and I'd carve soft rivers
into her very fine hair
that smelled only slightly of sweat.
With each mining shake of comb against scalp,
I'd break her aching day
into flakes we'd later brush from our clothes.
Now she sits in a kitchen chair,
her body cushioned, quiet,
none of those interesting creaks or pops
we laugh at because we hate them,
the proof of our aging.
Her scalp is quiet, too—
no more patient demands
or Charge Nurse attitudes
to dig up and sweep away.
These days, she looks for insurance payments
instead of good, strong veins,
but someone still has to bleed, she says.
I replace the wide, plastic teeth
with my fingers and she tells me
I get my hands from my father.

The back of my head
is like the back of hers.
I find the raised mole
in the place it's always been.

Harvard

In 7th grade Latin, I watched you scrape
plaque from the bottom row of your crooked teeth
with your thumbnail—longer than boys should wear—
then show the build-up— a pile visible
from the back of the room— to your ace.
He immediately tried to outdo you.
The teacher, with her cartoonish red hair
and lipstick-feathered mouth, continued
the lesson about eggs, her disgust shown
only in lips puckered into an
abused asshole.

I think your father was a doctor
and I'm sure your mother was a lawyer.
I remember your silence in English
when John, the dumb, fat, redneck
questioned the reality of the Cosbys.
I was never really sure why you were
named after an Ivy League school.
I think you told us why once,
but I didn't pay too much attention.

Our hormones made Latin class funny.
I tried not to angle my smile your way.
You were not cute and were dorky.
Your saving grace was your friend Aundrá,
who kept you anchored in New Jack Swing
and the hip-hop Nashville always got late.
You had a high waist and awkward booty

and walked on your tippy-toes like a horse.
Your nerdiness could not outweigh
your parents' comfortable wealth and so
you never seemed to dress very well, but
you always smelled like Tide detergent,
even if it faded your black khakis gangrene.
Your elbows and knees were often ashy.
Your father was maybe a doctor,
your mom probably a lawyer.
Your younger sister dressed well.
Was it because you were a boy
that you were so haphazard with your looks?
Maybe you were on that Einstein tip,
too caught up in your own genius to care.
No one talked about your grooming.
Everyone liked you 'cause you were goofy.
You made us all laugh with your silly puns.

You died in a motorcycle crash
during your first year at Stanford.
An only son, a rebellious cliché.
Aundrá gave me the news during spring break,
our freshman year. I thought he'd cry.
He lost his scholarship to FAMU.
His parents made him come home after that.
We don't know what happened to your sister.
I think of you during toothpaste commercials
and whenever I defend Cliff and Clair.

Athena of Nashville

One day I'll split my father's skull
and he will see me as a warrior.

Men will chase me, paint my skirts gold.

My father's appetites will shrink him.

I was born armored against his loss,
but my shield hangs too loosely.

When Sirens Sound but There Is No War

Sometimes the darkness edges in
at eleven a.m.
Trees become frenzied,
their limbs throwing themselves
away, out, up for mercy.
An empowered wind picks up
voices of the violent dead.
Nowhere is safe.
The awful beauty can land anywhere.

Let's stay outside,
bodies humming with leaden anticipation,
watch electricity crash
in demented rhythm.
The animals stop,
obeying the rage gusting through town,
and their silence bleeds into others.
Everything refuses to breathe.
An exhalation signals
a call, a shift in direction.
Heaven funnels its evil to earth.

Task complete,
the devil beats his wife.
Sighs mingle with hot rain.
The sun nods weakly, exhausted,
relieved.

Plump

There are no corners to my body.
I am round, round, round.
Sweet words slide off me,
collect at my feet.
I reach for them when I want
to remember softness away from my skin,
but the words have spoiled.

The sphere of my flesh protects me
from too much
yet leaves me open.
Everything is a circle—
the need, need, need comes back,
like fingers to mouth.

I can find me in paintings trapped in museums,
velvet-roped, untouchable.
Look how they used to love the full-hipped.
How strange they were.

The Wraith

She entered beneath my hairline,
chewed bits of me away.
I fed her your mouth, hands,
but it did little.
Food did less.
My skin stretched and filled,
yet she hungered all the time,
and my eyes emptied.

You wondered at my fullness,
gave your skin to mine,
but this thing inside me
thought it all too thin,
so she reached between,
pulling at the fat of us
until that, too, was hollowed.

Compound

The first few pounds
were happy-dating fat—
the dinner-to-impress dates,
the couch-movie snacks,
snuggle-only Sundays.
His face filled out some, sure.
He finished two push-ups
and looked twenty-five again.
Then he was gone—gone—
but the salty-sweets stayed.
They held tight while I read,
pillows the only company at my back.
Soon my belly bent the waistband,
and I hid, wanting to be gone, too.

Mama suggested body briefers.
Gran'mama would've called them girdles.
Stores list them as smoothers, shapers.
My friends pulled me from home once.
I wore a shaper-briefer-girdle;
later vomited chicken wings and Johnnie Walker.
But I had a waist again, you see.

Why can't I be like everyone else
with life monsters who
suck the happy fat from them,
leave them looking like
poets smoking black cigarettes?
My wraith feeds me
until I am twice what I am,
until I am twice gone.

To Be a Nymph

You were no god
to pretty yourself up
in a shower of gold
or a crown of sun.
You shifted the world with snarl,
and I changed my name to Daphne,
froze myself in bark.

Hide

Men on the street whisper
that I should give myself time,
that the boys will come around,
but I am not a golden thing.

I do not shine.

I lace myself in unpretty
to remain dim and hidden.
It scratches me, cuts a groove.
If I peel it away,
I don't know
what will hurt more—
its loss
or remaining unseen.

The Boy with the Freckles

His name was a kiss to say:
a soft opening of the mouth,
a quick move of the tongue.
And his face—a Seurat painting.

The freckles against his lips were
evidence of Cupid's stings,
that trickster making this boy's mouth
a distraction, a constant target.

The constellation on his left cheek
holds your name
when his mouth no longer can.

the promise

It was ten minutes after three,
and a half-moon gave us privacy.
He ran with his body low to the ground,
before stopping in front of the statue—
a supplicating Jesus.
He bent to one knee, head down, then stood and crossed himself
before racing back to the car, his face more shadowed
than that of the granite Savior's. As he settled into the seat,
he raised his pinky, the one next to his ring,
and made me swear I'd never tell.

The Professor

He sent me messages
from his honeymoon.
Each electronic love note
cost fifty cents a minute.
He must really love me
to send such sweet little nothings.

Mistress

He opened my mouth
and laid on my tongue a story.

His wife doesn't like
to do certain things,

and I let it slip into my throat,
let him squeeze my shoulder

and say, "good girl,"
when it was all gone.

Tourists

We chose the city and hotel at random.
You had research as an excuse.
I said I was visiting a friend.
The museum's heat was too high.
I could smell your deodorant working,
the artificial freshness of soap hitting my nose
every time you pulled at the neck of your shirt
trying to find a masculine way to cool yourself.
You touched the tattoo at my waist.

I don't remember the exhibit at all.

In the room,
the white sheets made you sigh.
You traced the edges of my body,
a skyline tourists collect,
proof of their adventures.

Adams Morgan, Washington, D.C. (January, 2003)

I.   *The Common Share*

He was a wild-haired thing—
a man so slight she wondered
if he used all that hair to keep himself anchored.
A trucker hat—John Deere—
somehow rested in the center
of the fro's frizzing spirals.
A drunken, lopsided smile shined from his face
with no particular target,
and she pressed closer to the wall,
knowing if he ever smiled fully,
with intention, at her,
she'd have to find her own means of escape.

II.   *Timheri*

Easing farther into the throb of bodies,
she sought to hide the increasing lack of rhythm in
her loosening limbs.
Soon slim fingers slipped through her belt loops.
She turned to distance herself
but her body stuttered back in place, against him.
Her soggy brain registered
the perched cap and unfocused smile,
and now the heat of his palms directed her sway.

They didn't speak.
No fumbling compliments
to yellow-brick-road the journey.
Belt buckle to curve,
riddims and beer synced their bodies.

Hoodoo

He asked her if, during her time in New Orleans,
she'd learned anything he wasn't sure he wanted to know.
Had she ever carved three x's into a certain woman's headstone?
Was there a special ingredient in her homemade pasta sauce?
Every night he checked beneath their pillows,
and every morning, he was careful with his discarded facial hair.
Pleased that his southern roots went deep,
she tried to reassure him as best she could,
but every now and then, she let a few things slip—
carefully-worded thoughts that burned the edges of his brain,
as if someone had charmed his shampoo.

Backsliders

I slip five dollars from your wallet
and walk to the corner store.
In the morning
we can blame our nausea
on wine from bottles that unscrew.

Thin.

We have grown thin;
our conversations worn and repetitive—
a favorite 45 skipping on the one note
we sing well.

You want comfort,
so I hold you,
the embrace gaunt
like a poet of failed sonnets.

Apologies are worthless,
stilted words rearranged and shifted
like magnetic poetry:
best reviewed when drunk.

I think I read in a magazine
that we should take a trip together,
maybe renew our vows.

The cat steps delicately
from her litter box.

Learning Photography

I take pictures of you but don't develop them.
You laugh because I want to use film.
I like the thought of you stuck, tightly wound,
dependent on toxins to bring your smile into color.
The contemporary one, you take instant pictures,
images of me appearing in the palm of your hand
more quickly than I would like. You show them to me,
laugh, again, at my grudging expressions,
then erase me, I mean, those pictures,
claiming that *photogenic* is a state of mind.
You don't have the patience to teach me about lighting
or filters or the law of thirds, so I learn on my own,
and let you flip through my album,
let you touch my cellophaned memories.

for e.

Our eyes open too early
for a Saturday morning.
Too accustomed to weekday alarms,
we talk to the ceiling.
The phone rings.
You turn your back for privacy's sake.
My girlfriend tells me her husband gets dumber by the minute.
I place my hand on the center of your spine.
Skinny men are always so warm.
The incoming sun fires up the copper beneath your brown.
I disconnect the call and settle my nose
between your shoulder blades.
"You smell like soap and salad," I say.
You mumble something about vegetable-based
glycerin soap, and I count fourteen
random hairs poking through your skin.
I pluck them gently,
tease you about the voodoo doll I'll one day make.
You wince only once.
I kiss the hurt,
knowing I will remember the taste
and smell of you
later,
when I am alone.

Fireflies

I've left behind the mason jars of childhood,
and now I capture fireflies beneath my skin,
waiting for someone who understands
the glow and fade and glow. and fade.

*

Remember the false habitats—
a few blades of green,
maybe a twig, a splash of water,
and the punctured tin tops for air?
The lightnin' would slow then stop,
so we'd tilt and shake and thump,
unable to acknowledge that
what we'd put inside would never be enough.

*

I can be bright again.
Let me lift my wings.

Clouds that Follow

Old folks say
not to bring anything baby
into the house until she's born.
I didn't listen.

None of it will be there next time.

He was patient, at first,
perhaps afraid to touch me.
As months passed,
confusion grew,
then his anger,
but I won't lose him, too.

We went to the park
and found animals in the clouds,
like children do,
or new lovers.
At home, his hands rediscovered me,
and to my surprise,
a menagerie had gathered
in the ceiling over our bed.

Najah

You pulled yourself away,
announcing your life with good-bye.
In silence, I hold my breath,
pretend my fluttering pulse is yours.
I think you would've been a girl.

Blackberry Winter

Our mouths should be covered
in a balloon bouquet of purple-black sweetness,
our feet bare, flat in grass—
but today, the morning leaves shake with frost,
and we curl our toes.
Two days ago, we were warm,
laughing at the sight of our pale legs,
sun-starved and stubbly.
We lounged on the porch,
ignoring the bare lawn.
I shaved my legs in a basin;
you ran your hand up, up, up,
called me a country wench.
Now we are here,
whispering excuses to remain still.

If Wishes Were Horses

Envy rides me,
and I am broken, trembling
beneath its mastery.
A quick squeeze of my ribs,
and I'm off,
chasing the gilded trophy.
When my hair looks like hers,
when I lose what makes me dimple,
when my teeth are perfect-perfect,
I'll win the prize of you.

Stand beside me.
Toss blankets of flowers over me.
When everyone is gone,
coo private words
and rest your forehead to mine.
Close the door. Lock me away.
I'll wait for you in the morning.

Former Sundays

I miss the midnight blossom of your mouth,
kissing you the moment
your bedtime minty freshness begins to flatten.
Your surfacing stubble would sound harsher than it felt.
Sometimes a stray outside would set off the motion lights,
and your eyes would silver, watching me.
The memories aggravate most
when the sun rises on Sundays.
We used to move to the living room,
project movies on the sheet you'd fashioned into a screen.
We'd doze over the documentaries you chose,
laugh so hard we had to rewind my selections.
We'd laser-tag the cat into a frenzy.
She wouldn't know which lap to rest in
so she'd stretch across us both,
purring as if the moment would never end.

Déjà Vu

I've met you before,
but you don't remember.
Now we are uneven strangers,
eyes freeze-tagging
in the home of a connecting friend.
I don't know why I am surprised
when you stand next to me,
pretending to review hors d'oeuvres
and desserts.
You want to tell me I look familiar,
but the line is older than your re-soled boots.
I am quiet, waiting.
You want to try the mixed berry compote
that seems to have been stirred too well.
I encourage you,
deciding to pass on something
that looks like early summer bird poo.
You laugh and
your smile comets through me.
The tail-end of its promise warms my face.
You ask my name, very softly,
the sibilance once heard in Eden.

Inglewood

The wires above our heads
make a funny noise,
like the audible panic
in a fly's desperate attempt
to avoid its sealed-window death.
Some say the wires bring death
as they buzz electricity into our homes.
How many cakes and lasagnas
did we make last year
for those cancer left behind?
Look at all of our boys stamped Special Ed.
They grow tired
of homework bleeding with mistakes
so they learn to stay home
and lean against those utility poles,
their skin reclaiming the reds and blues
of school days mistrusted.
And when those boys are gone,
away from here,
we toss their shoes in the air,
watch them land on the wires
some say started it all,
those power lines pushing our boys away.

Wonder Woman, Vol 1 #230: The Claws of Internet Porn

He'd wait until I was asleep.

> *I spun in circles, wearing spangled panties.*

At least the downloadable women looked like me,
       or were shaped like me.

> *I hovered, invisible.*

He was under a lot of stress, he said.

> *I rescued men trained to be stupid.*

The help I could be did not include asking questions,

> *I tied them up with the truth.*

or needing his hands in soft places.

> *I changed my hair, and no one knew me.*

an aubade of sorts

You have flimsy curtains.
I can watch the sky,
its ink fading from last night's story.
In your sleep, you sense my countdown
and anchor me with a leg.
The mushrooming light helps me study you,
the dark blond hair of your arm across me,
the vellum of you marked with my scratchings.
You asked for them when I tried to be polite.
You're the only one, you said.
When you open your eyes,
I see a blue I never wanted.
I smile from the doorway.

Mythological

Last week, a woman called me a witch,
told me don't ignore the conjurer within.
The year before that,
a lover, red-headed and guttural,
hung the word *hag* between us,
said I sat on his chest
too often in the night,
took his breath,
made him want to go over.

A country boy once poisoned me
with his pretty, pretty mouth,
but I remained on this side.
He would wake us both,
the second best part of him
inside the seventh best part of me,
said I kept walking in his dreams.

I have crashed men against me,
my waves lapping up their wrecked offerings.
They have no wax to save themselves,
but I have the rope, golden sometimes,
to bind them.

The Quest for Immortality

Will you write about this? Us?
I'd rather keep you
between the flickering lids of sleep
where you will be pretty and blurred.
There, your plum-tight skin pops.
I am Lilith, but dark, pressing you down.
The ground is purple with us.
The animals you named taught you well:
I will keep you beneath me forever.
My knees press a symphony from you.
Your face doesn't look like you,
but I see the teeth in your open mouth.
If I put you in a poem,
the neediness will soften you,
leave you pale.

Framboise

It's a raspberry-red lip gloss made special with a French
   name.
You like it, think it tastes like summer
when all that mattered was moving between smiles.
You don't like goodbyes,
so we keep them silent,
but your mouth has become fancy with me,
deeply red now, like pomegranate fingertips.
Kiss me again.
Take more fruit of me.
It means you have to come back.

Tornado Chaser

I'll ink a twister beneath my breast.
For the few who'll see it,
I'll tell them it's a tribute to Tennessee,
but it'll be for you—
the way you darken my life with clumsy elegance.
Your path is never the same
yet you always end up here,
ripping foundations with a howl.
Inside you,
you are calm and quiet and make me believe in God.

Blue Bottles

Blue bottles clink
from the bushes outside,
but that doesn't stop you.
You count the grains of salt
on the door's threshold
then step over them.
Once inside, you pull trinkets
from their hiding spaces,
asking me to remember.
My showers are cold—
no steam to reveal
the notes you traced into the mirror.
A laundry service comes now,
college-age boys earning pocket change
to collect my things.
You see, I must avoid your sock
the machine once ate then decided to re-gift me,
tucking it between my towels,
their fresh rain scent absorbing
the tang of my grief.

Code Switch

Forty hours every week,
we use kiln-fired voices
sealed with the flames of respectability.
Our words are careful, high-pitched.
We have to let them know they are safe.

At home
we cool our voices until
we can color them with us.
Your tired eyes follow me
as I remove the day.
Don't talk about them.
Don't bring them inside.
Hug me. Touch my neck.
Circle it.
Now press.
Press.
You are safe here.
Let me know the same.

Dive Bar

The stranger kisses me, and I think I like it.
The single-stall bathroom has walls filled
with people's need for eternity.
He puts a hand against my neck
just as I find your handwriting, our names.
He rocks his hips into me for attention.
I don't have a marker to cross out "forever,"
but this temporary heat should peel it away,
erase it.

Lakefront

We'd fought until we fell on each other,
not knowing how else to end it.
The next afternoon, the river, swollen with May,
crashed against the levee and sprayed our legs.
We overlooked the stink of it,
grateful for its cool,
for each other's quiet.
You tossed bits of sausage to
menacing seagulls.
The newspaper beneath our crawfish and shrimp
flapped the fear I was too ashamed to show.
You pulled me onto your chest
and gave me a kiss on the cheek
as a charm of protection.
I slept for a bit,
the beat of who you were, that day,
drowning out the danger circling above us.

White Boy Hunting

We lacquer ourselves in
pussy pinks and rent-paying reds,
fluff our hair to maximum 'fro.
They want to touch it—kinky and soft.
We keep our dancing simple
but our hair isn't the only thing
soft with tricks.
Their faces sharpen and warm,
the pulls from their beer lengthen.
They have no problem dating black girls.
Halle and Zoë are so hot.
We stay quiet,
let them buy us drinks,
brush against our surprising skin.
These aren't the ones we want—
their nervous babbling proves them unfit.
We throw them back, check our glosses,
let them be content with the tale of their almost-capture.

Keepsake

I will stick you between the pages of
Song of Solomon—
Mother Toni's or King James'.
No navel,
or one filled with wine.
My own is crooked,
unworthy of ink, but
touch mouth to me.
I will make you a praise song.

Revenant

I don't visit graveyards after the funerals—
The buried don't care.

Every time I pass a man on the street,
his card table full of scented oils,
I sniff Egyptian Musk,
wonder at the clean stink of love,
wonder if you feel me touch our tombstone.

Tea with Vanya

He uses his hunting knife
to peel a Cara Cara orange.
The rind drops to the table in a single twirl.
He has the hands of a pianist turned to hockey.
His fingers will carry the sweetness
for the rest of the night,
candied and bitter.
I close my mouth over the edge of my cup and drink.
I've used too much honey, but I won't say anything.
He tears apart the orange, offers some to me.
I hold a blink too long.
The fruit feels luxurious in this small kitchen
with the upstairs neighbor who paces heavily
each time we laugh or sigh too loudly.
When I open my eyes,
he has shaped the peel into a sphere again.
If I take it from him, it will collapse,
but I know he'll cup his hands around mine,
show me how to make it stay.

The Drummer

Your hands are small.
You tense,
waiting for me to call you dainty,
but you are inelegant in your smallness,
your walk a jagged cardiogram
of the unending music in your head.

Men I can carry on my back hunt me.
They want to overwhelm themselves,
watch me spill over.

I keep you blind,
night cloth against your eyes,
your calloused hands pinned.
Your pale, northeastern skin
becomes the fireworks of sunrise
beneath my heavy palms.

What music do you hear
when your gratitude erupts?

Underwater

for Ivan

He wants to take me to the ocean,
but first I have to learn to swim better.
He's afraid to drown in my panic
if I lose myself to the sapphire.

They say my people
collectively fear the ocean.
The bejeweled graveyard pierces our every birth.

He is from a place of night and snow,
where I don't exist beyond a TV screen.
Yet here we are,
his red beard beneath my brown hands.
We teach each other new ways to breathe.

He wants to take me to the ocean.
Don't pull me under, he says.

Dandelion Wish

You kiss me and I am reminded
of the pinch and pull
of tasting honeysuckle.
Summer is an unfinished thing
without a stamen sliding
across lips to fall to the ground, spent.

My shirt lands softly, and
your mouth covers my navel.
I inhale memories—
cornstarch in my belly button,
healing chigga bites
from rolling down too many
plush Nashville hills,
simply for the sake of dizziness,
breathlessness.

Voice faint against my ear,
you ask a question.
My hair clings to your goatee,
like the cookaburrs that
stuck to socks after climbing
through sticka bushes,
looking for baby tomatoes
to squish and throw as weapons.

Your voice has deepened,
lost its cosmopolitan polish
until we are here—

no bespoke suits,
no peeptoe heels,
our names—
two syllables in the city—
become three
in the country of our skins.
We are the boy
who picked strawberries
from his backyard,
whose hair was left uncut
too long, those curls
the only halo you'd ever have.
We are the girl
who raced barefoot through thick grass,
who felt the false comfort of
a tornado's silence raise
forearm hairs as signals.
You—
umbered like new Virginia tobacco—
me—
your Tennessee whiskey woman—
here—
in the country of our skins,
no plum seeds sprouting
in our bellies,
only the familiar, welcoming fear
of going home.
home.

I blew away dandelions to find you.

The Thought that Counts

Men press their lips to the length of my scar.

It's how they tell me I'm still pretty.
I feel those kisses with open eyes.
The flesh is dead there.

If I lower lashes to cheek,
I won't know what they're doing,
can't sigh like they want,
but I want to close my eyes and hide.

These men with their mouths against my unfeeling skin
hope to heal me with their touch,
but they belong to no king,
have no king's horses,
and I have already put myself back together.

Self-Portrait

I have a favorite picture of myself.
This is important because I do not
like myself in pictures.
It's a self-portrait. A selfie.
I was drunk, hence the grin.
You'd made me laugh
so the grin is honest
and lives in my eyes.
You were coming through the door
while I tried to find my best angle.
My double chin is a bitch to hide.

In the picture,
I can see your bookshelf,
the green chevron pillow on your couch.
You are there and not there
in this favorite moment of me.

I don't know where you are now.

#ebony

I love your skin and hair.
You're beautiful.
You don't take shit from anyone.
Have you ever been with a white guy?
I love the contrast of our skin.
And you always smell so good.
It's just different from white girls.
They're so boring.
They're so weak.
You say what you mean.
Is it true that black guys don't go down?
Is it true that black guys have big dicks?
I'm okay but nothing scary.
I've never been with a black woman before.
I've always wanted to.
I love black women.
You're so strong.
It seems like it takes a lot to handle you.
You're probably used to black guys.
Do you like to take control a lot?
I'm really good with my mouth.
You can do anything you want to me.
You can do anything.
Anything.
I've always loved black women.

A Black Woman Came to Yoga Today

It was her first time.
She didn't speak to me
when I didn't speak to her.
She couldn't hold many poses.
She must be so jealous of me.

No one tried to help her.
Should I try to help her?
No, she's angry.
I can tell by the way she didn't answer
when I didn't ask her.
I feel so bad.

My flexible white-girl body
reminds her of everything she's not.

It makes me want to cry.

The Threat of Pretty

The men tell you you'll be pretty one day,
when all your features settle.
A compliment, an insult, a threat.

These men want you to talk to them
on the bus, at the corner store.
They smell of beer and gasoline.

You've never liked talking to strangers,
especially men whose eyes
want someone to pay
for the dirt under their fingernails.

These men say your pretty hasn't arrived
yet they follow you home,
their hands active in pockets with no change.

What will they do when your face pleases them?

Derrick

When spring arrived,
our parents sent us outside.
Their jobs were misery
and they didn't want to hear
school news that led to more requests for money.
Derrick kept us neighborhood kids entertained.

He would settle a needle into Patti LaBelle,
flattened for the world to consume.
The vinyl spun like her hair,
grooved and firm and hypnotizing.
The music stretched into the street,
and we'd watch Derrick's frontyard singalongs.
He matched Patti note for note,
his shoulder shimmy ecstatic.

Derrick choreographed our outdoor concerts.
Our Soul Train lines were his catwalk.
His nails and lips glowed
in a way mine weren't allowed to.
Why couldn't I wear makeup if he could?
In answer, my mother would turn away.

A mean boy lived by the alley.
He told us in rough, fascinating language
all the things girlbodies were made for.
His hands were rough on Derrick's sister.
Her cries stopped the flow of Patti.
Derrick stepped past the bushes bordering their house.
In one hand was a thick, knobby branch.
In the other was a gun,
stubby and silver, at home in his palm.
Which one do you want upside your head?
Don't make me make a mess.

The Blue

Ivan, again

Ocean mouth of salt and soothing
Your bones I have worried smooth
and collected on window sills
Seaweed sheets against the tongue
Sharp memory of you
breaking against me
Breaking away

Avon for Life

I never played in my mother's makeup
but her scented lotions were my treasure to find.
Midnight blue jars with gold tops and white cream inside,
a thick champagne rubbed into the skin
to take her away from nurse's shoes and pastel scrubs.
She would order the jars from women at work,
flipping through catalog pages,
looking for red-lined items as extra treats.

Catalogs make you feel special.
Everything can be yours,
specially delivered to you.
You are more than your job, Mama.
You are more than the five remaining dollars
after the bills are paid.
You deserve to smell like a tropical fantasy,
not the harsh clinic soap that strips your skin and leaves it pale.

The lotions— "perfumed skin softeners" —had names
like Imari, Night Magic, Odyssey.
The musk and amber and spice were too heavy for me then,
but I understand them now.
There is a woman here, heady and blooming.

Acknowledgments

Bill Brown, Dr. Mona Lisa Saloy, Dr. Gloria Wade-Gayles, Pearl Cleage, Dr. Bettye Parker-Smith, Dr. Chandra Mountain, Dr. Yolanda W. Page, Gabrielle Pina, Dr. Kalenda Eaton, Alisha Cheek, Cynthia Harris, Rashad Mobley, Donnie Seals, Tracy Clayton, Stacia Brown, Kelley Gueye, Tyesha Willis, Brent Hughes, Andrea Chung, D'Gregory Craig, Tabitha Mason-Elliott, Koku K., Susan Caldwell, Monica Parran, PostBourgie, Justin Roberts, Stephanie Pruitt-Gaines, Roxane Gay, Daniel Mallory Ortberg, Nicole Cliffe, Ashley Ford, Bim Adewunmi, Eleanor Kagan, Julia Furlan, Driadonna Roland, Chantal Follins, Kima Jones, Dr. LaToya Watkins: you all have nurtured and provided for me in various ways, from helping me learn the craft of writing to exposing me to literary greats to giving me a place to rest my head and everything in between. You've supported me with encouraging words, good meals, and full-belly laughs. I've learned so much about being true to myself through all of you. Thank you.

Many of these poems were created at the University of Southern California, the Napa Valley Writers' Conference and at the Callaloo Creative Writing Workshop under the guidance of Nan Cohen, the late C.D. Wright, Major Jackson, and Vievee Francis.

To the various branches of the Puckett and Perkins families, I love you.

Thank you to all the men I loved and those I wanted to love, to those who saved my life and those who tried to ruin it.

Nichole Perkins is a writer from Nashville, Tennessee. She is a 2016 Callaloo Creative Writing Fellow in poetry, the Audre Lorde Fellow at the 2017 Jack Jones Literary Arts Retreat, and a 2017 BuzzFeed Emerging Writers Fellow.